Fluõ | **Travel**

# LYON

COLOR MAP

**Lyon Color Map**
By Isaac M. Harland

First Edition: March 2019

**Scale** / 1:7500

| 100m

| 500ft

# At a Glance

| | |
|---|---|
| **Country** | France |
| **Region** | Auvergne-Rhône-Alpes |
| **Native Name** | Lyon |
| **Established** | 43 BC |
| **Language** | French |
| **Currency** | Euro (EUR) |
| **Plug Type** | C, E (230V) |
| **Driving** | Right-hand |
| **Population** | 513,275 |
| **Area** | 47.87 sq.kms |
| **Postal Code** | 69123 |
| **Area Code** | +(33)4 |
| **Timezone** | CET (+1) |
| **Timezone DST** | CEST (+2) |

Map 3

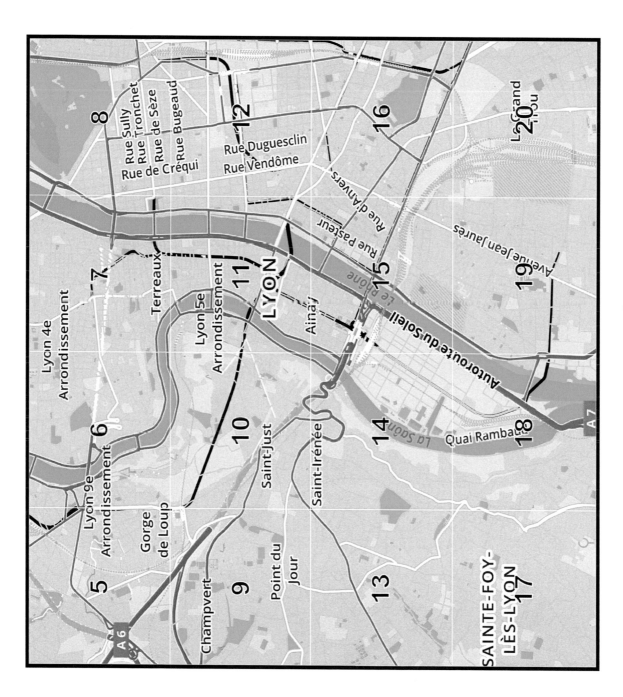

**Map Overview**

| | | | |
|---|---|---|---|
| Archaeological site | | Information |
| Artwork | | Jewish synagogue |
| Atm | | Kiosk |
| Bar | | Library |
| Bicycle rental | | Lighthouse |
| Biergarten | | Memorial |
| Buddhist temple | | Monument |
| Bus station | | Museum |
| Bus stop | | Muslim mosque |
| Cafe | | Parking |
| Camping site | | Peak |
| Car rental | | Pharmacy |
| Cave entrance | | Picnic site |
| Chalet | | Playground |
| Church / Monastery | | Police |
| Cinema | | Post office |
| Courthouse | | Prison |
| Department store | | Pub |
| Drinking water | | Railway |
| Dry cleaning | | Restaurant |
| Embassy | | Shinto temple |
| Fast food | | Sikh temple |
| Ferry terminal | | Sports centre |
| Fire station | | Supermarket |
| Fountain | | Taxi |
| Fuel | | Telephone |
| Golf course | | Theatre |
| Hindu temple | | Toilets |
| Hospital | | Townhall |
| Hostel | | Traffic signals |
| Hotel | | Windmill |

SAINT-IRÉNÉE

14

10

Rue de la Quarar

Montée de Choulans

Montée de Choulans

Quai Fulchiron

Autoroute du Sole

Montée Saint-Laurent

Rue du Fort Saint-Irénée

Rue de l'Aube

Rue Sœur Bouvier

Rue Sœur Bouvier

Boulevard des Castors

Rue Marcel Achard

Rue Claude Jusseaud

Rue des Castors

Avenue Debrousse

Chemin de Fontanières

Quai des Etroits

Quai Rambaud

Quai Rambaud

Rue Claudius Collonge

La Saône

Cours Suchet

Rue Bichat

P

Rue Nicolas Berthet

Place Général Delfosse

Poste ERDF Rue Bichat

Parc du Brûlet

Rue Denuzière

Decarpentrie

Allée Paul Scherrer

Rue Seguin

Pl l'Hip

Avenue Vallioud

Quai Rambaud

Cours Bayard

Cours Charlemagne

Rue Georges Clemenceau

Rue Casimir Périer

educ
Gier

Jardin d'Erevan

Rue Denuzière

Rue Denuzière

Chemin Léon Favre

Chemin de Fontanières

Quai Jean-Jacques Rousseau

Quai Antoine Riboud

Place Nautique

Place Nautique

Confluence

Marché-gare

Rue Casimir P

La Saône

Quai Rambaud

18

Cours Charlemagne

Rue Smith

Esplanade

Made in the USA
San Bernardino, CA
10 May 2019